MW00873369

'2021

DAILY AFFIRMATIONS FOR
CHRISTIAN TEEN GIRLS

Daily Affirmations
FOR CHRISTIAN TEEN GIRLS

INSPIRATION, MOTIVATION, AND POSITIVITY

LISA ZECH

ROCKRIDGE
PRESS

Interior and Cover Designer: Lisa Schreiber
Art Producer: Samantha Ulban
Editor: Eun H. Jeong
Production Editor: Ruth Sakata Corley
Production Manager: Riley Hoffman

Copyright Page: All images used under license © Shutterstock and iStock. Author photo courtesy of Mandy Zech

Paperback ISBN: 978-1-63807-081-8 | eBook ISBN: 978-1-63807-700-8

R0

For Hannah and California Rose,
may you always be beautiful, inside
and out. And for Nora, let Jesus lead
you, my precious baby girl.

Introduction

Do you ever think about how strange the world is? It's beautiful and mysterious, too; I've always wanted to climb the Cliffs of Moher in Ireland, hike the bamboo trails of Hawaii, and just spend time with the beauty God created. But sometimes, it can be hard to find beauty in our day-to-day lives—especially when you're a teenager, living in a world where things, people, relationships, and places (and, I might add, bodies) are constantly changing.

When I was a teenager, I sometimes struggled to find the beauty in daily life. That's why, when I was 16, I started a social media community so that my friends and I could encourage one another as Christian teen girls. It slowly morphed into an online ministry, but in the beginning, it was just for fun. My friends and I would share verses to help one another through tough things like learning how to be bold in our faith, how to feel confident in awkward situations at school or church, and how to react to our feelings about guys and all the other new experiences we had to navigate.

I am hoping that this book can be like that online community for you. Each day, you'll read a new important scripture, along with a short daily affirmation that you can carry at the forefront of your thoughts as you learn, worship, or hang out with friends. You can read each entry in the morning to give you encouragement during your day or at night, when you just need a moment to rest, unwind, and hear God's voice. The affirmations are like little messages that will help you remember the verse you read. They are there to encourage, inspire, and empower you, to help you feel strong in your relationship with Jesus and find beauty in your day.

Jesus wants to be your closest friend, to help guide you through this unpredictable season of your life. And I'm praying that this book can help you with that. I wrote out a quick prayer for you to read now, just to kick us off on this journey.

Lord, thank you for wanting to be my closest friend. Teach me to know you more, and show me your heart, your thoughts, and your desire for my life as I go through this book. Help these short messages to be big encouragements in my life and to remind me of you and of how close you are to me throughout the day. I love you, Jesus.

Amen.

I am so excited to go on this journey with you! And I can't wait to see how this little book inspires you on your walk with Jesus.

Affirmations

|1|

Then they cry out to the Lord in their trouble, And He brings them out of their distresses. He calms the storm, So that its waves are still. Then they are glad because they are quiet; So He guides them to their desired haven.

PSALMS 107:28–30 NKJV

God rescues me from any trouble and guides me to my desired haven.

|2|

I, yes I, am the One and Only, who completely erases your sins, never to be seen again. I will not remember them again. Freely I do this because of who I am!

ISAIAH 43:25 TPT

As soon as Jesus forgives me, He casts my wrongdoings away and does not keep a record.

| 3 |

Have you forgotten that your body is now the sacred temple of the Spirit of Holiness, who lives in you? You don't belong to yourself any longer, for the gift of God, the Holy Spirit, lives inside your sanctuary. . . . so by all means, then, use your body to bring glory to God!

1 CORINTHIANS 6:19–20 TPT

I honor Him with my body and in all that I do because Jesus lives in me.

| 4 |

Finally, all of you should be of one mind. Sympathize with each other. Love each other as brothers and sisters. Be tenderhearted, and keep a humble attitude. Don't repay evil for evil. Don't retaliate with insults when people insult you. Instead, pay them back with a blessing.

1 PETER 3:8–9 NLT

When people hurt my feelings, I don't retaliate but instead treat them the same way Jesus treats me.

| 5 |

Do not love this world nor the things it offers you. . . .
For the world offers only a craving for physical
pleasure, a craving for everything we see. . . . These
are not from the Father, but are from this world. And
this world is fading away, along with everything that
people crave. But anyone who does what pleases
God will live forever.

1 JOHN 2:15–17 NLT

I seek to please Jesus instead of
craving the sinful things of this world
because He has set me apart.

| 6 |

"For I know the plans I have for you," says the Lord.
"They are plans for good and not for disaster, to give
you a future and a hope. In those days when you
pray, I will listen. If you look for me wholeheartedly,
you will find me."

JEREMIAH 29:11–13 NLT

God listens to me when I call and has
awesome plans for my life!

| 7 |

This is my command—be strong and courageous!
Do not be afraid or discouraged. For the Lord your
God is with you wherever you go.

JOSHUA 1:9 NLT

God makes me strong and courageous;
I have nothing to be afraid of.

| 8 |

But blessed are those who trust in the Lord and have
made the Lord their hope and confidence. They are
like trees planted along a riverbank, with roots that
reach deep into the water.

JEREMIAH 17:7–8 NLT

The Lord is where my confidence
comes from; I will not be moved!

| 9 |

For you created my inmost being; you knit me together in my mother's womb. I praise you because I am fearfully and wonderfully made; your works are wonderful, I know that full well.

PSALMS 139:13–14 NIV

Jesus has made me perfect with His own hands, so I love my body without judgment.

| 10 |

My child, do not reject the Lord's discipline, and don't get angry when he corrects you. The Lord corrects those he loves, just as parents correct the child they delight in.

PROVERBS 3:11–12 NCV

Jesus disciplines me in love so that I can learn, grow, and keep trying my best at everything.

| 11 |

Don't copy the behavior and customs of this world, but let God transform you into a new person by changing the way you think. Then you will learn to know God's will for you, which is good and pleasing and perfect.

ROMANS 12:2 NLT

Jesus is transforming me so I will be less like the world and more like Him.

| 12 |

Give careful thought to the paths for your feet and be steadfast in all your ways. Do not turn to the right or the left; keep your foot from evil.

PROVERBS 4:26–27 NIV

I pay attention to the steps I take so that I stay on the road God is leading me down.

| 13 |

Be happy with those who are happy, and weep with those who weep. Live in harmony with each other. Don't be too proud to enjoy the company of ordinary people. And don't think you know it all!

ROMANS 12:15–16 NLT

I am an example of Christ when I treat others the way He would treat them.

| 14 |

For you are my refuge, a high tower where my enemies can never reach me. I shall live forever in your tabernacle; oh, to be safe beneath the shelter of your wings!

PSALMS 61:3–4 TLB

I am safe when I go to Jesus; He is my hiding place!

| 15 |

No temptation has overtaken you except such as is common to man; but God is faithful, who will not allow you to be tempted beyond what you are able, but with the temptation will also make the way of escape, that you may be able to bear it.

1 CORINTHIANS 10:13 NKJV

God always provides a path out of temptation. I will be vigilant in order to find it.

| 16 |

For I am persuaded that neither death nor life, nor angels nor principalities nor powers, nor things present nor things to come, nor height nor depth, nor any other created thing, shall be able to separate us from the love of God which is in Christ Jesus our Lord.

ROMANS 8:38–39 NKJV

Nothing and no one can separate me from God's powerful love.

| 17 |

For the Lord your God is living among you. He is a mighty savior. He will take delight in you with gladness. With His love, He will calm all your fears. He will rejoice over you with joyful songs.

ZEPHANIAH 3:17 NLT

Jesus takes delight in me; He calms all my fears and makes me joyful.

| 18 |

Let your speech always be with grace, seasoned with salt, that you may know how you ought to answer each one.

COLOSSIANS 4:6 NKJV

I speak with grace and wisdom when I let Jesus show me what to say.

| 19 |

Charm is deceptive, and beauty does not last; but a woman who fears the Lord will be greatly praised.

PROVERBS 31:30 NLT

My heart desires to please God, so I set aside concerns about my outward appearance.

| 20 |

Since you have been raised to new life with Christ, set your sights on the realities of heaven, where Christ sits in the place of honor at God's right hand. Think about the things of heaven, not the things of earth.

COLOSSIANS 3:1–2 NLT

When I get stuck in my own head, I ask God to center my thoughts on things that are good.

| 21 |

We can rejoice, too, when we run into problems and trials, for we know that they help us develop endurance. And endurance develops strength of character, and character strengthens our confident hope of salvation.

ROMANS 5:3–4 NLT

When I am struggling in life, I remember that God uses those trials to make me stronger!

| 22 |

I will set nothing wicked before my eyes; I hate the work of those who fall away; It shall not cling to me.

PSALMS 101:3 NKJV

When I'm online or on social media, I steer clear of anything that isn't honoring God.

| 23 |

And we know that in all things God works for the good of those who love him, who have been called according to his purpose.

ROMANS 8:28 NIV

I go through the day with confidence because God is working on my circumstances and will provide a good outcome for every difficulty I face.

| 24 |

Above all, clothe yourselves with love, which binds us all together in perfect harmony. And let the peace that comes from Christ rule in your hearts. For as members of one body you are called to live in peace. And always be thankful.

COLOSSIANS 3:14–15 NLT

I live in peace with those around me because Jesus is in my heart.

| 25 |

Be of good courage, and He shall strengthen your heart, all you who hope in the Lord.

PSALMS 31:24 NKJV

The Lord strengthens my heart when I hope in Him.

| 26 |

These things I have spoken to you, that in Me you may have peace. In the world you will have tribulation; but be of good cheer, I have overcome the world.

JOHN 16:33 NKJV

I am fearless because God has already overcome everything the world could try to hinder me with.

| 27 |

Don't let anyone think less of you because you are young. Be an example to all believers in what you say, in the way you live, in your love, your faith, and your purity.

1 TIMOTHY 4:12 NLT

Just because I am young doesn't mean I can't be a good influence on others.

| 28 |

Therefore, if anyone is in Christ, he is a new creation; old things have passed away; behold, all things have become new.

2 CORINTHIANS 5:17 NKJV

I am a completely new person in Christ because of His sacrifice for me; I no longer live for myself, but for Him.

| 29 |

Don't be concerned about the outward beauty of fancy hairstyles, expensive jewelry, or beautiful clothes. You should clothe yourselves instead with the beauty that comes from within, the unfading beauty of a gentle and quiet spirit, which is so precious to God.

1 PETER 3:3–4 NLT

I nurture my inner beauty, knowing that my heart and spirit is precious to God.

| 30 |

Oh, the joys of those who do not follow the advice of the wicked, or stand around with sinners, or join in with mockers. But they delight in the law of the Lord, meditating on it day and night. They are like trees planted along the riverbank, bearing fruit each season. Their leaves never wither, and they prosper in all they do.

PSALMS 1:1–3 NLT

When I refuse to give into peer pressure and instead decide to live a godly life, Jesus makes me joyful and prosperous!

| 31 |

Those who live according to the flesh have their minds set on what the flesh desires; but those who live in accordance with the Spirit have their minds set on what the Spirit desires. The mind governed by the flesh is death, but the mind governed by the Spirit is life and peace.

ROMANS 8:5–6 NIV

When I let the Holy Spirit rule my thoughts, I have peace in my life.

| 32 |

Come to me, all you who are weary and burdened, and I will give you rest. Take my yoke upon you and learn from me, for I am gentle and humble in heart, and you will find rest for your souls.

MATTHEW 11:28–29 NIV

When I feel worried and burdened, Jesus gives me rest and so much comfort.

| 33 |

Many, O Lord my God, are your wonderful works
Which you have done; And your thoughts toward
us Cannot be recounted to you in order; If I would
declare and speak of them, They are more than can
be numbered.

PSALMS 40:5 NKJV

The Lord thinks about me more than I
could ever know.

| 34 |

God blesses you when people mock you and perse-
cute you and lie about you and say all sorts of evil
things against you because you are my followers.
Be happy about it! Be very glad! For a great reward
awaits you in heaven.

MATTHEW 5:11–12 NLT

Jesus is on my side and has blessings in
store for me no matter what others say
or do against me.

| 35 |

For we are His workmanship, created in Christ Jesus
for good works, which God prepared beforehand
that we should walk in them.

EPHESIANS 2:10 NKJV

I am God's handiwork, and He has lots
of good things for me to accomplish
with my life!

| 36 |

"My grace is enough for you. When you are weak,
then my power is made perfect in you." . . . So I am
happy when I have weaknesses, insults, hard times,
sufferings, and all kinds of troubles. All these things
are for Christ. And I am happy, because when I am
weak, then I am truly strong.

2 CORINTHIANS 12:9–10 ICB

God uses my weakness to show how
strong He is and how strong He can
make me.

| 37 |

Honor your father and your mother, that your days may be long upon the land which the Lord your God is giving you.

EXODUS 20:12 NKJV

When I honor my parents or guardians, God blesses me in ways I might not even know about or understand.

| 38 |

For as the heavens are high above the earth, So great is His mercy toward those who fear Him; As far as the east is from the west, So far has He removed our transgressions from us.

PSALMS 103:11–12 NKJV

I am so important to Jesus that He has forgiven me for all my past wrongs.

| 39 |

For the grace of God has appeared that offers salvation to all people. It teaches us to say "No" to ungodliness and worldly passions, and to live self-controlled, upright and godly lives in this present age.

TITUS 2:11–12 NIV

I am strong in God's grace and can say "No" to things of the world.

| 40 |

He who dwells in the secret place of the Most High Shall abide under the shadow of the Almighty. I will say of the Lord, "He is my refuge and my fortress; My God, in Him I will trust."

PSALMS 91:1–2 NKJV

I trust Jesus with my whole life because He will always protect me!

| 41 |

Confess your trespasses to one another, and pray for one another, that you may be healed. The effective, fervent prayer of a righteous man avails much.

JAMES 5:16 NKJV

When I confess and pray about my wrongdoings, my wounds are healed and I am free.

| 42 |

But let all those rejoice who put their trust in You; Let them ever shout for joy, because You defend them; Let those also who love Your name Be joyful in You.

PSALMS 5:11 NKJV

I am joyful because of Jesus and because He defends me from any circumstances that try to threaten me.

| 43 |

Since you were precious in My sight, You have been honored, And I have loved you; Therefore I will give men for you, And people for your life. Fear not, for I am with you.

ISAIAH 43:4–5 NKJV

God would do anything for me, as I am precious in His sight.

| 44 |

But I say, love your enemies! Pray for those who persecute you! In that way, you will be acting as true children of your Father in heaven.

MATTHEW 5:44–45 NLT

With God's strength, I can love people who I don't like, and who dislike me.

| 45 |

That is what the Scriptures mean when they say, "No eye has seen, no ear has heard, and no mind has imagined what God has prepared for those who love him." But it was to us that God revealed these things by his Spirit. For his Spirit searches out everything and shows us God's deep secrets.

1 CORINTHIANS 2:9–10 NLT

God has amazing things in store for me; no matter what I face presently, I know He has bigger things planned for me ahead.

| 46 |

God wants us to grow up, to know the whole truth and tell it in love—like Christ in everything. We take our lead from Christ, who is the source of everything we do. He keeps us in step with each other. His very breath and blood flow through us, nourishing us so that we will grow up healthy in God, robust in love.

EPHESIANS 4:15–16 MSG

God is always helping me grow into the strong and healthy woman that He needs me to be.

| 47 |

I will both lie down in peace, and sleep; For You alone, O Lord, make me dwell in safety.

PSALMS 4:8 NKJV

I rest well, knowing that God is working on my behalf and keeping me safe.

| 48 |

The Lord's justice will dwell in the desert, his righteousness live in the fertile field. The fruit of that righteousness will be peace; its effect will be quietness and confidence forever.

ISAIAH 32:16–17 NIV

The Lord's goodness gives me an inner confidence; I know He is faithful.

| 49 |

Don't worry about anything; instead, pray about everything. Tell God what you need, and thank him for all he has done. Then you will experience God's peace, which exceeds anything we can understand. His peace will guard your hearts and minds as you live in Christ Jesus.

PHILIPPIANS 4:6–7 NLT

I give God all my anxieties and worries because He gives me surpassing peace.

| 50 |

Flee the evil desires of youth and pursue righteousness, faith, love and peace, along with those who call on the Lord out of a pure heart.

2 TIMOTHY 2:22 NIV

I chase after righteousness and choose friends who do the same.

| 51 |

And above all things have fervent love for one another, for "love will cover a multitude of sins." Be hospitable to one another without grumbling.

1 PETER 4:8–9 NKJV

God gives me love for my family all the time, even when I feel grumpy or annoyed.

| 52 |

Serve the Lord with gladness; Come before His presence with singing. Know that the Lord, He is God; It is He who has made us, and not we ourselves; We are His people and the sheep of His pasture.

PSALMS 100:2–3 NKJV

I am the Lord's daughter, so I will serve Him with joy and gladness!

|53|

But thanks be to God, who gives us the victory through our Lord Jesus Christ. Therefore, my beloved brethren, be steadfast, immovable, always abounding in the work of the Lord, knowing that your labor is not in vain in the Lord.

1 CORINTHIANS 15:57–58 NKJV

I am steadfast and immovable in the face of challenges and temptation, because God has given me victory in Jesus!

|54|

Your kingdom is an everlasting kingdom, And Your dominion endures throughout all generations. The Lord upholds all who fall, And raises up all who are bowed down.

PSALMS 145:13–14 NKJV

The Lord will last forever, and He will always be there to keep me from falling.

| 55 |

But the wisdom that is from above is first pure, then peaceable, gentle, willing to yield, full of mercy and good fruits, without partiality and without hypocrisy. Now the fruit of righteousness is sown in peace by those who make peace.

JAMES 3:17–18 NKJV

God gives me the wisdom I need to deal with anything that may try to hinder me.

| 56 |

Let not steadfast love and faithfulness forsake you; bind them around your neck; write them on the tablet of your heart. So you will find favor and good success in the sight of God and man.

PROVERBS 3:3–4 ESV

Being loving and faithful in all my relationships helps me glorify Jesus through them.

| 57 |

So get rid of all the filth and evil in your lives, and humbly accept the word God has planted in your hearts, for it has the power to save your souls. But don't just listen to God's word. You must do what it says. Otherwise, you are only fooling yourselves.

JAMES 1:21–22 NLT

When I am faithful and obey God's Word, I will be saved from evil.

| 58 |

"God is mighty, but he does not despise anyone! He is mighty in both power and understanding."

JOB 36:5 NLT

I am always understood and protected by my God!

|59|

I pray that your hearts will be flooded with light so that you can understand the confident hope he has given to those he called—his holy people who are his rich and glorious inheritance.

EPHESIANS 1:18 NLT

I have such powerful and confident hope in Jesus for everything I need.

|60|

My honor and salvation come from God. He is my mighty rock and my protection. People, trust God all the time. Tell him all your problems. God is our protection.

PSALMS 62:7–8 ICB

God is my source of protection, and I can trust Him with anything!

| 61 |

They [women] should wear decent and appropri-ate clothing and not draw attention to themselves by the way they fix their hair or by wearing gold or pearls or expensive clothes. For women who claim to be devoted to God should make themselves attrac-tive by the good things they do.

1 TIMOTHY 2:9–10 NLT

I don't need to dress for attention; I honor God with the good things I do.

| 62 |

Trust in the Lord, and do good; Dwell in the land, and feed on His faithfulness. Delight yourself also in the Lord, And He shall give you the desires of your heart.

PSALMS 37:3–4 NKJV

God gives me my heart's desires when I delight in Him!

|63|

You are the light of the world—like a city on a hilltop that cannot be hidden. . . . In the same way, let your good deeds shine out for all to see, so that everyone will praise your heavenly Father.

MATTHEW 5:14, 16 NLT

Jesus makes me a bright light and a godly example to others around me.

|64|

Oh, give thanks to the Lord, for He is good! For His mercy endures forever.

PSALMS 106:1 NKJV

God's mercy toward me is unending; He gives me grace even when I feel undeserving.

| 65 |

A merry heart does good, like medicine, But a
broken spirit dries the bones.

PROVERBS 17:22 NKJV

I choose to be joyful so I can bless
those around me.

| 66 |

Yet the Lord longs to be gracious to you; therefore
He will rise up to show you compassion. For the Lord
is a God of justice. Blessed are all those who wait
for Him!

ISAIAH 30:18 NIV

Patience comes easily to me because
God always shows Himself to be
gracious.

| 67 |

Don't envy sinners, but always continue to fear the Lord. You will be rewarded for this; your hope will not be disappointed.

PROVERBS 23:17–18 NLT

I don't ever need to be jealous of sinful people; God has bigger plans for me.

| 68 |

Do not worry about your life, what you will eat or what you will drink; nor about your body, what you will put on. . . . Look at the birds of the air, for they neither sow nor reap . . . yet your heavenly Father feeds them. Are you not of more value than they?

MATTHEW 6:25–26 NKJV

I am so valuable to God and He will provide, so I can let go of my worries and stress.

| 69 |

Do nothing out of selfish ambition or vain conceit.
Rather, in humility value others above yourselves,
not looking to your own interests but each of you to
the interests of the others.

PHILIPPIANS 2:3–4 NIV

I am called to care about others the
same way I care about myself.

| 70 |

. . . do not worry about how or what you should
speak. For it will be given to you in that hour what
you should speak; for it is not you who speak, but
the Spirit of your Father who speaks in you.

MATTHEW 10:19–20 NKJV

Whether I'm at school or work, I speak
with confidence because God speaks
through me!

| 71 |

Training your body helps you in some ways, but serving God helps you in every way. Serving God brings you blessings in this life and in the future life, too.

1 TIMOTHY 4:8 ICB

Serving God is the greatest thing I could ever accomplish in my life!

| 72 |

God can do anything, you know—far more than you could ever imagine or guess or request in your wildest dreams! He does it not by pushing us around but by working within us, his Spirit deeply and gently within us.

EPHESIANS 3:20 MSG

God is in me and can do anything for me—more than I can possibly imagine!

| 73 |

For you are a people holy to the Lord your God. The Lord your God has chosen you out of all the peoples on the face of the earth to be his people, his treasured possession.

DEUTERONOMY 7:6 NIV

I am more valuable than all worldly things because I am treasured by God!

| 74 |

But godliness with contentment is great gain. For we brought nothing into the world, and we can take nothing out of it. For the love of money is a root of all kinds of evil. Some people, eager for money, have wandered from the faith and pierced themselves with many griefs.

1 TIMOTHY 6:6–7, 10 NIV

When I put Jesus first, I find contentment within any circumstance.

| 75 |

Do not judge others, and you will not be judged. For you will be treated as you treat others.

MATTHEW 7:1–2 NLT

I treat others the way I want to be treated and never judge them for being different.

| 76 |

Do everything without grumbling or arguing, so that you may become blameless and pure, "children of God without fault in a warped and crooked generation." Then you will shine among them like stars in the sky.

PHILIPPIANS 2:14–15 NIV

When I have a good, cheerful attitude in life, I shine like the stars!

| 77 |

He has made everything beautiful in its time. He has also set eternity in the human heart; yet no one can fathom what God has done from beginning to end.

ECCLESIASTES 3:11 NIV

God is making me beautiful, inside and out, in His perfect timing.

| 78 |

Blessed are the pure in heart, for they will see God.

MATTHEW 5:8 NIV

God is honored when I have pure intentions.

| 79 |

She is clothed with strength and dignity, and she laughs without fear of the future.

PROVERBS 31:25 NLT

I am not afraid of what lies ahead, because God gives me courage about the future.

| 80 |

Cling to your faith in Christ, and keep your conscience clear. For some people have deliberately violated their consciences; as a result, their faith has been shipwrecked.

1 TIMOTHY 1:19 NLT

My faith is secure when I stand strong in my convictions.

| 81 |

Your righteousness is like the mighty mountains, your justice like the ocean depths. You care for people and animals alike, O Lord. How precious is your unfailing love, O God! All humanity finds shelter in the shadow of your wings.

PSALMS 36:6–7 NLT

Knowing Jesus's unfailing love for me gives me shelter from any insecurities.

| 82 |

As in water face reflects face, So a man's heart reveals the man.

PROVERBS 27:19 NKJV

My heart is reflected in my character, so I strive to bring honor to God.

| 83 |

But Christ died for us while we were still sinners. In this way God shows his great love for us.

ROMANS 5:8 ICB

God loves me so much that even when I sin, He redeems me.

| 84 |

All your children shall be taught by the Lord, and great shall be the peace of your children.

ISAIAH 54:13 ESV

My heart and mind are open to Jesus because the most important things I can learn in life come from Him.

| 85 |

How beautiful are the feet of those who preach the gospel of peace, Who bring glad tidings of good things!

ROMANS 10:15 NKJV

When I spread the words of Jesus,
I bring beauty to those around me.

| 86 |

For by grace you have been saved through faith, and that not of yourselves; it is the gift of God, not of works, lest anyone should boast.

EPHESIANS 2:8–9 NKJV

There is nothing I can do to deserve God's love and grace; it is His free gift to me.

| 87 |

But since you excel in everything—in faith, in speech, in knowledge, in complete earnestness and in the love we have kindled in you—see that you also excel in this grace of giving.

2 CORINTHIANS 8:7 NIV

I look forward to showing God's grace to others, because they might need it just as much as I do.

| 88 |

Let us draw near to God with a sincere heart and with the full assurance that faith brings. . . . Let us hold unswervingly to the hope we profess, for he who promised is faithful.

HEBREWS 10:22–23 NIV

When I speak truthfully with God during my quiet time with Him, He fills me with faith.

|89|

I will praise you, Lord my God, with all my heart; I will glorify your name forever. For great is your love toward me; you have delivered me from the depths, from the realm of the dead.

PSALMS 86:12–13 NIV

God has delivered me from so much, including death, so I WORSHIP Him!

|90|

In his kindness God called you to share in his eternal glory by means of Christ Jesus. So after you have suffered a little while, he will restore, support, and strengthen you, and he will place you on a firm foundation.

1 PETER 5:10 NLT

I am calm and courageous even when I experience hardship, knowing that God will restore me and make me secure.

| 91 |

For in him all things were created: things in heaven and on earth, visible and invisible, whether thrones or powers or rulers or authorities; all things have been created through him and for him.

COLOSSIANS 1:16 NIV

I have been created so that Jesus can use me for His glory and to spread His love to others.

| 92 |

Yet you, Lord, are our Father. We are the clay, you are the potter; we are all the work of your hand.

ISAIAH 64:8 NIV

I am being shaped and molded by the Lord; I'm His masterpiece.

| 93 |

God's dwelling place is now among the people,
and he will dwell with them. They will be his people,
and God himself will be with them and be their God.
"He will wipe every tear from their eyes. There will be
no more death" or mourning or crying or pain.

REVELATION 21:3–4 NIV

God comforts me; He wipes my tears
and gives me hope for tomorrow.

| 94 |

"He himself bore our sins" in his body on the cross, so
that we might die to sins and live for righteousness;
"by his wounds you have been healed." For "you were
like sheep going astray," but now you have returned
to the Shepherd and Overseer of your souls.

1 PETER 2:24–25 NIV

I always return to Jesus, because He
heals me from my sin.

| 95 |

You make known to me the path of life; you will fill me with joy in your presence, with eternal pleasures at your right hand.

PSALMS 16:11 NIV

God leads me and fills me with joy and His pleasure.

| 96 |

You will keep in perfect peace those whose minds are steadfast, because they trust in you. Trust in the Lord forever, for the Lord himself, is the Rock eternal.

ISAIAH 26:3-4 NIV

When I trust in the Lord and keep my mind focused on Him, I have peace.

| 97 |

Commit to the Lord whatever you do, and he will establish your plans.

PROVERBS 16:3 NIV

I am determined and empowered, knowing that Jesus blesses my efforts.

| 98 |

Preach the word; be ready in season and out of season; reprove, rebuke, and exhort, with complete patience and teaching.

2 TIMOTHY 4:2 ESV

Jesus gives me the boldness and graciousness to share His Word with my friends.

| 99 |

Above all else, guard your heart, for everything you do flows from it.

PROVERBS 4:23 NIV

Jesus gives me the ability to protect my heart from negative thoughts and bad influences.

| 100 |

If your gift is to encourage others, be encouraging. If it is giving, give generously. If God has given you leadership ability, take the responsibility seriously. And if you have a gift for showing kindness to others, do it gladly.

ROMANS 12:8 NLT

I have so many gifts, and I can use them all to bless others!

|101|

Blessed are those who find wisdom, those who gain understanding, for she is more profitable than silver and yields better returns than gold. She is more precious than rubies; nothing you desire can compare with her.

PROVERBS 3:13–15 NIV

I prioritize wisdom over my daily worries and pressures.

|102|

I asked the Lord for help, and he answered me. He saved me from all that I feared. Those who go to him for help are happy, and they are never disgraced.

PSALMS 34:4–5 NCV

I seek the Lord with all my heart when I am afraid.

|103|

We who are strong in faith should help the weak with their weaknesses, and not please only our-selves. Let each of us please our neighbors for their good, to help them be stronger in faith.

ROMANS 15:1–2 NCV

God helps me encourage others when they are feeling weak and discouraged.

|104|

So don't worry, because I am with you. Don't be afraid, because I am your God. I will make you strong and will help you; I will support you with my right hand that saves you.

ISAIAH 41:10 NCV

I trust the Lord to provide for me and give me strength.

| 105 |

Blessed is the one who fears the Lord always, but whoever hardens his heart will fall into calamity.

PROVERBS 28:14 ESV

When I have a humble heart, I stay away from evil.

| 106 |

When I said, "My foot is slipping," your unfailing love, Lord, supported me. When anxiety was great within me, your consolation brought me joy.

PSALMS 94:18–19 NIV

Right before I fall or slip up, God saves me and comforts me with joy.

| 107 |

Control yourselves and be careful! The devil is your enemy. And he goes around like a roaring lion looking for someone to eat. Refuse to give in to the devil. Stand strong in your faith. You know that your Christian brothers and sisters all over the world are having the same sufferings you have.

1 PETER 5:8–9 ICB

When I resist the devil and remember I'm not alone, my faith is strong.

| 108 |

I leave you peace; my peace I give you. I do not give it to you as the world does. So don't let your hearts be troubled or afraid.

JOHN 14:27 NCV

The peace that God gives me can outlast any temporary peace the world may offer.

|109|

Keep your lives free from the love of money, and be satisfied with what you have. God has said, "I will never leave you; I will never abandon you."

HEBREWS 13:5 NCV

I am free from jealousy and envy because I know God provides everything I need.

|110|

How terrible it will be for people who call good things bad and bad things good. They think darkness is light and light is darkness. They think sour is sweet and sweet is sour.

ISAIAH 5:20 ICB

I know better than to think that the evil things I see in movies and on social media are okay for me to do.

| 111 |

Do not stir up nor awaken love until it pleases.

SONG OF SOLOMON 8:4 NKJV

I don't need to rush my love life; God will awaken it in His time.

| 112 |

But the Spirit produces the fruit of love, joy, peace, patience, kindness, goodness, faithfulness, gentleness, self-control.

GALATIANS 5:22–23 NCV

God's Spirit gives me the gifts I need to build a good character.

| 113 |

God wants you to be holy and to stay away from sexual sins. He wants each of you to learn to control your own body in a way that is holy and honorable.

1 THESSALONIANS 4:3–4 NCV

God gives me the power to control my body and my sexual desires, if only I ask Him to!

| 114 |

We do not dare to compare ourselves with those who think they are very important. They use themselves to measure themselves, and they judge themselves by what they themselves are. This shows that they know nothing.

2 CORINTHIANS 10:12 NCV

I love myself for who God made me to be, without judgment or comparison.

| 115 |

Do you think I am trying to make people accept me? No, God is the One I am trying to please. Am I trying to please people? If I still wanted to please people, I would not be a servant of Christ.

GALATIANS 1:10 NCV

God is the only one whose approval I seek; I only want to please Him!

| 116 |

Likewise, you younger people, submit yourselves to your elders. Yes, all of you be submissive to one another, and be clothed with humility, for "God resists the proud, but gives grace to the humble."

1 PETER 5:5 NKJV

God is honored when I am humble and obedient to my elders.

| 117 |

May the Lord bless you and keep you. May the Lord show you his kindness and have mercy on you. May the Lord watch over you and give you peace.

NUMBERS 6:24–26 NCV

God is always on my side; He keeps me in His protection.

| 118 |

So avoid sorrow and sadness. Forget about all the bad things that happen to you. This is because the joys of youth pass quickly away.

ECCLESIASTES 11:10 ICB

I have a healthy, joyful outlook on life, knowing that each moment is precious.

| 119 |

Do all you can to live a peaceful life. Take care of your own business, and do your own work as we have already told you. If you do, then people who are not believers will respect you, and you will not have to depend on others for what you need.

1 THESSALONIANS 4:11–12 NCV

When I work hard and live peacefully, I gain respect in life.

| 120 |

But I am like an olive tree flourishing in the house of God; I trust in God's unfailing love for ever and ever.

PSALMS 52:8 NIV

God's love makes me flourish like a fruitful tree.

| 121 |

The Scriptures give us patience and encouragement so that we can have hope. May the patience and encouragement that come from God allow you to live in harmony with each other the way Christ Jesus wants.

ROMANS 15:4–5 NCV

I ask God for patience and peace, no matter how frustrated or stressed I am.

| 122 |

Happy is the person who trusts the Lord, who doesn't turn to those who are proud or to those who worship false gods.

PSALMS 40:4 NCV

I have happiness when I put my trust in God, not other people or things.

|123|

So put all evil things out of your life: sexual sinning, doing evil, letting evil thoughts control you, wanting things that are evil, and greed. This is really serving a false god.

COLOSSIANS 3:5 NCV

I won't give in to sin so that it can't control my life.

|124|

The Lord is kind and shows mercy. He does not become angry quickly but is full of love. The Lord is good to everyone; he is merciful to all he has made.

PSALMS 145:8–9 NCV

Jesus is slow to anger and full of love, so when I come to Him for help, I have nothing to fear.

| 125 |

So let's not get tired of doing what is good. At just the right time we will reap a harvest of blessing if we don't give up.

GALATIANS 6:9 NLT

God gives me the strength and perseverance to do what is right.

| 126 |

Everything the Lord does is right. He is loyal to all he has made. The Lord is close to everyone who prays to him, to all who truly pray to him.

PSALMS 145:17–18 NCV

When I pray to the Lord, He is close to me.

| 127 |

Therefore, since we are surrounded by such a huge crowd of witnesses to the life of faith, let us strip off every weight that slows us down, especially the sin that so easily trips us up. And let us run with endurance the race God has set before us.

HEBREWS 12:1 NLT

I continue forward and persevere, knowing that sin can't weigh me down.

| 128 |

Be joyful in hope, patient in affliction, faithful in prayer.

ROMANS 12:12 NIV

I am joyful and patient during hard times, because I know my faith is only growing stronger.

| 129 |

Now may the Lord direct your hearts into the love of God and into the patience of Christ.

2 THESSALONIANS 3:5 NKJV

Jesus is leading me to His love and His kind of patience.

| 130 |

But seek first his kingdom and his righteousness, and all these things will be given to you as well. Therefore, do not worry about tomorrow, for tomorrow will worry about itself. Each day has enough trouble of its own.

MATTHEW 6:33–34 NIV

I focus on today's challenges instead of worrying needlessly about the future, knowing that God provides.

|131|

No, O people, the Lord has told you what is good, and this is what he requires of you: to do what is right, to love mercy, and to walk humbly with your God.

MICAH 6:8 NLT

Jesus directs me to be humble, to be merciful, and to love doing what is right.

|132|

Do not be yoked together with unbelievers. For what do righteousness and wickedness have in common? Or what fellowship can light have with darkness?

2 CORINTHIANS 6:14 NIV

I am excited to surround myself with friends who want to lift one another up and live in the light of God.

| 133 |

Create in me a pure heart, O God, and renew a steadfast spirit within me. Do not cast me from your presence or take your Holy Spirit from me.

PSALMS 51:10–11 NIV

When my faith is weak and I need my spirit renewed, I look to Jesus and He restores me.

| 134 |

Always be joyful. Pray continually, and give thanks whatever happens. That is what God wants for you in Christ Jesus.

1 THESSALONIANS 5:16–18 NCV

Today I choose to be grateful and joyous, no matter what comes my way!

| 135 |

Cast your cares on the Lord and he will sustain you;
he will never let the righteous be shaken.

PSALMS 55:22 NIV

God sustains me when I am worried; I cannot be shaken.

| 136 |

I appeal to you, brothers and sisters, in the name of
our Lord Jesus Christ, that all of you agree with one
another in what you say and that there be no divi-
sions among you, but that you be perfectly united in
mind and thought.

1 CORINTHIANS 1:10 NIV

Through God, I can be a peacemaker and united with my family, friends, and peers.

| 137 |

Do not let any unwholesome talk come out of your mouths, but only what is helpful for building others up according to their needs, that it may benefit those who listen.

EPHESIANS 4:29 NIV

What I say matters, so I am intentional with my words, making sure that they are helpful and encouraging.

| 138 |

Commit your way to the Lord, trust also in Him, and He shall bring it to pass.

PSALMS 37:5 NKJV

If my emotions start taking control, I know that committing my heart to God will help me stay calm.

| 139 |

If you are wise and understand God's ways, prove it by living an honorable life, doing good works with the humility that comes from wisdom. But if you are bitterly jealous and there is selfish ambition in your heart, don't cover up the truth with boasting and lying.

JAMES 3:13–14 NLT

I prove that I walk in God's Spirit with my actions; I will never suppress my faith.

| 140 |

She speaks wise words and teaches others to be kind.

PROVERBS 31:26 NCV

God gives me wisdom and kindness to use in all my interactions.

|141|

Whatever you do, work heartily, as for the Lord and not for men, knowing that from the Lord you will receive the inheritance as your reward. You are serving the Lord Christ.

COLOSSIANS 3:23–24 ESV

I make sure that whatever I do today brings glory to Jesus, my best friend.

|142|

I can do all things through Christ, because he gives me strength.

PHILIPPIANS 4:13 NCV

God can accomplish anything in and through me, including all my own dreams and goals.

|143|

If you diligently obey the voice of the Lord your God . . . the Lord your God will set you high above all nations of the earth. And all these blessings shall come upon you and overtake you, because you obey the voice of the Lord your God.

DEUTERONOMY 28:1–2 NKJV

When I obey God's voice, He blesses me with everything I need in life.

|144|

Set a guard over my mouth, Lord; keep watch over the door of my lips.

PSALMS 141:3 NIV

I guard my speech, so that I only say things that are uplifting.

| 145 |

So, whether we are at home or away, we make it our aim to please [God].

2 CORINTHIANS 5:9 ESV

Jesus is my main priority, whether I am at school, home, or work.

| 146 |

Lord, you have been our home since the beginning. Before the mountains were born and before you created the earth and the world, you are God. You have always been, and you will always be.

PSALMS 90:1–2 NCV

When I am feeling insecure, all I need to do is remember that Jesus is my home and best friend.

| 147 |

Keep on loving each other as brothers and sisters.
Remember to welcome strangers, because some
who have done this have welcomed angels without
knowing it.

HEBREWS 13:1–2 NCV

I love others, even though they are
different from me, knowing that God
has created us all in His image.

| 148 |

Two are better than one, because they have a good
reward for their toil. For if they fall, one will lift up
his fellow. But woe to him who is alone when he falls
and has not another to lift him up!

ECCLESIASTES 4:9–10 ESV

When my friends and I work together,
we encourage and lift one another up.

| 149 |

If anyone believes in me, rivers of living water will flow out from that person's heart, as the Scripture says.

JOHN 7:38 NCV

I am confident instead of self-conscious because God's living, powerful Spirit is in me.

| 150 |

Dear friends, we should love each other, because love comes from God. The person who loves has become God's child and knows God.

1 JOHN 4:7 ICB

When it feels hard to love my family, God gives me love for them.

| 151 |

Come near to God, and God will come near to you. You are sinners. So clean sin out of your lives. You are trying to follow God and the world at the same time. Make your thinking pure.

JAMES 4:8 ICB

When I follow Jesus, I cleanse my life of sin and impurity.

| 152 |

You have not seen Christ, but still you love him. You cannot see him now, but you believe in him. You are filled with a joy that cannot be explained. And that joy is full of glory.

1 PETER 1:8 ICB

My faith makes me joyful, even when things at school and home are hard.

| 153 |

The unfolding of your words gives light; it imparts understanding to the simple.

PSALMS 119:130 ESV

I seek God's Word in the morning, because it gives me wisdom for the day.

| 154 |

A friend loves you all the time. A brother is always there to help you.

PROVERBS 17:17 ICB

I support and accept my friends, even when I don't feel like it, because I inspire them to do the same.

| 155 |

For I am the Lord, I do not change; Therefore you are not consumed, O sons of Jacob.

MALACHI 3:6 NKJV

Even though I'll get older and change, I know Jesus lives in me and will never change.

| 156 |

So we should stop doing things that belong to darkness and take up the weapons used for fighting in the light. Let us live in a right way, like people who belong to the day. We should not have wild parties or get drunk.

ROMANS 13:12–13 NCV

When I feel peer pressure to do the wrong thing, I use God's weapons to fight temptation.

| 157 |

Intelligent people are always ready to learn. Their ears are open for knowledge.

PROVERBS 18:15 NLT

When I put my mind to my schoolwork, Jesus gives me the wisdom and intelligence I need.

| 158 |

Jesus Christ is the same yesterday, today, and forever. So do not be attracted by strange, new ideas. Your strength comes from God's grace.

HEBREWS 13:8–9 NLT

Even when there is bad news, I am not discouraged by it because I know God never changes.

| 159 |

Lord our God, treat us well. Give us success in what we do; yes, give us success in what we do.

PSALMS 90:17 NCV

Jesus makes me successful at anything I set out to do.

| 160 |

Every good action and every perfect gift is from God. These good gifts come down from the Creator of the sun, moon, and stars, who does not change like their shifting shadows. God decided to give us life . . . so we might be the most important of all the things he made.

JAMES 1:17–18 NCV

All of my blessings are from God, especially my life, which is precious to Him!

| 161 |

All Scripture is breathed out by God and profitable for teaching, for reproof, for correction, and for training in righteousness, that the man of God may be competent, equipped for every good work.

2 TIMOTHY 3:16–17 ESV

The Bible is the compass for my life; through it, Jesus teaches me.

| 162 |

If we confess our sins, he is faithful and just to forgive us our sins and to cleanse us from all unrighteousness.

1 JOHN 1:9 ESV

When I do wrong, Jesus always forgives me and cleanses my heart.

| 163 |

But when the kindness and love of God our Savior was shown, he saved us because of his mercy. It was not because of good deeds we did to be right with him. He saved us through the washing that made us new people through the Holy Spirit.

TITUS 3:4–5 NCV

The good I try to do on my own can't save me; only God's mercy can do that.

| 164 |

Your word is a lamp to my feet and a light to my path.

PSALMS 119:105 ESV

I seek God's Word and let it guide me as I start and end my day.

| 165 |

My dear children, you belong to God and have
defeated them; because God's Spirit, who is in you, is
greater than the devil, who is in the world.

1 JOHN 4:4 NCV

Satan will try to make me stumble and
bring me down, but God is in me and
He is greater!

| 166 |

The Lord is my rock and my fortress and my deliv-
erer, my God, my rock, in whom I take refuge, my
shield, and the horn of my salvation, my stronghold.

PSALMS 18:2 ESV

Though friends, school, work, and
family will all change, God will always
be with me.

| 167 |

Do not be deceived: "Bad company ruins good morals."

1 CORINTHIANS 15:33 ESV

I make sure everyone I follow on social media is a good influence.

| 168 |

Before the mountains were brought forth, or ever you had formed the earth and the world, from everlasting to everlasting you are God.

PSALMS 90:2 ESV

God is at the beginning and end of my story; He is my rock.

| 169 |

Distress that drives us to God does that. It turns us around. It gets us back in the way of salvation. We never regret that kind of pain. But those who let distress drive them away from God are full of regrets, end up on a deathbed of regrets.

2 CORINTHIANS 7:10 MSG

I repent of my sins and do not let them control me or cause more regret.

| 170 |

Beloved, we are God's children now, and what we will be has not yet appeared; but we know that when he appears we shall be like him, because we shall see him as he is.

1 JOHN 3:2 ESV

I may not know where my life's journey is headed, but I know that Jesus is making me like Him so I can face my future.

| 171 |

The steadfast love of the Lord never ceases; his mercies never come to an end; they are new every morning; great is your faithfulness.

LAMENTATIONS 3:22–23 ESV

God has new plans and new mercy for me every morning, even before I wake.

| 172 |

And this world is fading away, along with everything that people crave. But anyone who does what pleases God will live forever.

1 JOHN 2:17 NLT

All the things and people I covet are fading; that's why I please Jesus, rather than people.

| 173 |

On the day I called, you answered me; my strength of soul you increased.

When I face new challenges, I know that God hears me and gives me strength.

| 174 |

We capture every thought and make it give up and obey Christ.

2 CORINTHIANS 10:5 NCV

I capture my thoughts before they cause damage and surrender them to Jesus.

| 175 |

O Lord, you have searched me and known me! You know when I sit down and when I rise up; you discern my thoughts from afar. You search out my path and my lying down and are acquainted with all my ways.

PSALMS 139:1–3 ESV

Jesus knows every single thing I am going to do in the day, even my thoughts and plans.

| 176 |

We know we love God's children if we love God and obey his commandments. Loving God means keeping his commandments, and his commandments are not burdensome.

1 JOHN 5:2–3 NLT

When I obey the Lord and his Word, I am loving Him and those around me!

| 177 |

As obedient children, do not be conformed to the passions of your former ignorance, but as he who called you is holy, you also be holy in all your conduct.

1 PETER 1:14–15 ESV

When I'm tempted by peers or outside influences, I remember to make God-honoring decisions.

| 178 |

How precious are your thoughts about me, O God. They cannot be numbered! I can't even count them; they outnumber the grains of sand! And when I wake up, you are still with me!

PSALMS 139:17–18 NLT

Even when I feel disappointed by my friends and family, I know Jesus is always thinking of me.

| 179 |

Whoever keeps his commandments abides in God,
and God in him. And by this we know that he abides
in us, by the Spirit whom he has given us.

1 JOHN 3:24 ESV

God proves that He lives in me when
I make choices that glorify Him.

| 180 |

Be sober-minded; be watchful. Your adversary the
devil prowls around like a roaring lion, seeking
someone to devour.

1 PETER 5:8 ESV

I am watchful and aware of
temptation, condemnation, and other
traps the devil sets in my life.

| 181 |

For it was fitting that he, for whom and by whom all things exist, in bringing many sons to glory, should make the founder of their salvation perfect through suffering.

HEBREWS 2:10 ESV

I do not fear struggles and failures; Jesus uses them to make me stronger in my faith.

| 182 |

Who may ascend into the hill of the Lord? Or who may stand in His holy place? He who has clean hands and a pure heart, who has not lifted up his soul to an idol, nor sworn deceitfully.

PSALMS 24:3–4 NKJV

Though it's easy to idolize fashion and trends, only Jesus is King of my heart.

|183|

Dear brothers and sisters, if another believer is overcome by some sin, you who are godly should gently and humbly help that person back onto the right path. And be careful not to fall into the same temptation yourself.

GALATIANS 6:1 NLT

I don't follow temptation; instead, I am fearless in talking to my friends about Jesus.

|184|

Lord, tell me your ways. Show me how to live. Guide me in your truth, and teach me, my God, my Savior. I trust you all day long.

PSALMS 25:4–5 NCV

Even when all I see around me is uncertainty and change, God shows me how to live.

| 185 |

One who is faithful in a very little is also faithful in much, and one who is dishonest in a very little is also dishonest in much.

LUKE 16:10 ESV

I am responsible and faithful with all the things God has blessed me with.

| 186 |

The Lord will fulfill his purpose for me; your steadfast love, O Lord, endures forever. Do not forsake the work of your hands.

PSALMS 138:8 ESV

God has a plan for my life, and He'll make sure I accomplish it.

| 187 |

But people are tempted when their own evil desire leads them away and traps them. This desire leads to sin, and then the sin grows and brings death.

JAMES 1:14–15 NCV

Sinful actions begin as thoughts; Jesus helps me abstain from temptation.

| 188 |

The Lord's name should be praised from where the sun rises to where it sets. The Lord is supreme over all the nations; his glory reaches to the skies.

PSALMS 113:3–4 NCV

I set aside time to worship Jesus in the morning and in the evening, every day, knowing that it glorifies God.

| 189 |

So we fix our eyes not on what is seen, but on what is unseen, since what is seen is temporary, but what is unseen is eternal.

2 CORINTHIANS 4:18 NIV

The difficult things that I might be facing right now are temporary, but God's plan is eternal!

| 190 |

What can I give the Lord for all the good things he has given to me? I will lift up the cup of salvation, and I will pray to the Lord.

PSALMS 116:12–13 NCV

God does not desire outward gifts; He simply wants my heart to be full of worship.

|191|

"So no weapon that is used against you will defeat you. You will show that those who speak against you are wrong. These are the good things my servants receive. Their victory comes from me," says the Lord.

ISAIAH 54:17 NCV

When people say bad things about me, I know God's Word is the only one that matters.

|192|

Therefore let us not pass judgment on one another any longer, but rather decide never to put a stumbling block or hindrance in the way of a brother.

ROMANS 14:13 ESV

I lead by example and strive to be a good influence for my friends and family.

| 193 |

Everything he does is good and fair; all his orders can be trusted. They will continue forever. They were made true and right.

PSALMS 111:7–8 NCV

I trust that anything God asks me to do is good and trustworthy.

| 194 |

For the word of God is living and active, sharper than any two-edged sword, piercing to the division of soul and of spirit, of joints and of marrow, and discerning the thoughts and intentions of the heart.

HEBREWS 4:12 ESV

God's Word shows me the areas of my life that need godly change.

| 195 |

When I was a child, I spoke like a child, I thought like a child, I reasoned like a child. When I became a man, I gave up childish ways.

1 CORINTHIANS 13:11 ESV

My body is changing and so are my actions; I am a woman of God.

| 196 |

We do live in the world, but we do not fight in the same way the world fights. We fight with weapons that are different from those the world uses. Our weapons have power from God that can destroy the enemy's strong places.

2 CORINTHIANS 10:3–4 NCV

God's Spirit gives me the power to tear down the sinful strongholds in my life.

| 197 |

A light shines in the dark for honest people, for those who are merciful and kind and good. It is good to be merciful and generous. Those who are fair in their business will never be defeated.

PSALMS 112:4–6 NCV

Even when people are different from me, it is important to treat them fairly and with love and mercy.

| 198 |

For your Maker is your husband, the Lord of hosts is his name; and the Holy One of Israel is your Redeemer, the God of the whole earth he is called.

ISAIAH 54:5 ESV

When it comes to romantic relationships, I look to Jesus first and foremost for love and protection.

| 199 |

Bless the Lord, O my soul, and forget not all his benefits, who forgives all your iniquity, who heals all your diseases, who redeems your life from the pit, who crowns you with steadfast love and mercy, who satisfies you with good so that your youth is renewed like the eagle's.

PSALMS 103:2–5 ESV

Jesus does so much to love and save me each day, so I bless Him with all I have!

| 200 |

You love right and hate evil, so God has chosen you from among your friends; he has set you apart with much joy.

HEBREWS 1:9 NCV

God gives me joy because I love and follow His ways above my own selfish ways.

| 201 |

It is better to trust the Lord than to trust people. It is better to trust the Lord than to trust princes.

PSALMS 118:8–9 NCV

What I see on social media can be really misleading; it's better to only trust in Jesus.

| 202 |

I am the Lord, and there is no other. I create the light and make the darkness. I send good times and bad times. I, the Lord, am the one who does these things.

ISAIAH 45:6–7 NLT

There will be many seasons in my life, good and bad, but God will carry me through them all.

| 203 |

So Jesus said to the Jews who believed in him, "If you continue to obey my teaching, you are truly my followers. Then you will know the truth, and the truth will make you free."

JOHN 8:31–32 NCV

Knowing God's truth, instead of just following popular opinion, sets me free from the enemy's lies.

| 204 |

The Lord is my light and my salvation; whom shall I fear? The Lord is the stronghold of my life; of whom shall I be afraid?

PSALMS 27:1 ESV

When I feel intimidated, Jesus makes me brave and gives me the ability to feel brave around others.

| 205 |

Therefore, having put away falsehood, let each one of you speak the truth with his neighbor, for we are members one of another.

EPHESIANS 4:25 ESV

I speak truthfully with my friends and family, knowing I build good character.

| 206 |

Wait for the Lord; be strong, and let your heart take courage; wait for the Lord!

PSALMS 27:14 ESV

Even though my life plans are uncertain, I wait patiently and pray for Jesus to guide and direct my path.

| 207 |

Now the Lord is the Spirit, and where the Spirit of the Lord is, there is freedom.

2 CORINTHIANS 3:17 ESV

God's Spirit in my heart gives me freedom from strongholds of fear and discouragement.

| 208 |

Therefore we must pay much closer attention to what we have heard, lest we drift away from it.

HEBREWS 2:1 ESV

My life has a lot of distractions but remembering God's promises keeps me anchored to Him.

|209|

Therefore, as you received Christ Jesus the Lord,
so walk in him, rooted and built up in him and
established in the faith, just as you were taught,
abounding in thanksgiving.

COLOSSIANS 2:6–7 ESV

I am grateful for what Jesus has done
and pursue Him passionately.

|210|

In the last days there will come times of difficulty. For
people will be lovers of self, lovers of money, proud,
arrogant, abusive, disobedient to their parents,
ungrateful, unholy, heartless, unappeasable, slander-
ous, without self-control, brutal, not loving good . . .
lovers of pleasure rather than lovers of God, having
the appearance of godliness, but denying its power.
Avoid such people.

2 TIMOTHY 3:1–5 ESV

Since I am a Christian, I make sure to
avoid worldly and evil influences or
friends.

| 211 |

When you were stuck in your old sin-dead life, you were incapable of responding to God. God brought you alive—right along with Christ! Think of it! All sins forgiven, the slate wiped clean, that old arrest warrant canceled and nailed to Christ's cross.

COLOSSIANS 2:14 MSG

All my past and present mistakes are nailed to the cross; Jesus gives me victory!

| 212 |

Finally, be strong in the Lord and in the strength of his might. Put on the whole armor of God, that you may be able to stand against the schemes of the devil. For we do not wrestle against flesh and blood, but against the rulers, against the cosmic powers over this present darkness.

EPHESIANS 6:10–12 ESV

Many people and situations will try to make me stumble, but I stand strong in Jesus.

| 213 |

I am the Lord; there is no other God. I have equipped you for battle, though you don't even know me, so all the world from east to west will know there is no other God.

ISAIAH 45:5–6 NLT

God shows Himself to be powerful through the victories He gives me in my life.

| 214 |

And "don't sin by letting anger control you." Don't let the sun go down while you are still angry, for anger gives a foothold to the devil.

EPHESIANS 4:26–27 NLT

If I stay angry, sin can creep into my life; I resolve my issues before they control me.

| 215 |

Little children, you are from God and have overcome them, for he who is in you is greater than he who is in the world.

1 JOHN 4:4 ESV

Jesus is stronger than anything that will try to overtake me in this world.

| 216 |

Get rid of all bitterness, rage, anger, harsh words, and slander, as well as all types of evil behavior. Instead, be kind to each other, tenderhearted, forgiving one another, just as God through Christ has forgiven you.

EPHESIANS 4:31–32 NLT

Jesus gave me a way of life that is forgiving and kind, just like He is toward me!

| 217 |

For in Christ lives all the fullness of God in a human body. So you also are complete through your union with Christ, who is the head over every ruler and authority.

COLOSSIANS 2:9–10 NLT

God has complete authority in this life, so He will have the final say in my future.

| 218 |

God showed how much he loved us by sending his one and only Son into the world so that we might have eternal life through him. This is real love—not that we loved God, but that he loved us and sent his Son as a sacrifice to take away our sins.

1 JOHN 4:9–10 NLT

When I am feeling alone, I remember that Jesus gave up eternity to have me close to Him.

| 219 |

See to it that no one takes you captive by philosophy and empty deceit, according to human tradition, according to the elemental spirits of the world, and not according to Christ.

COLOSSIANS 2:8 ESV

I will not be easily swayed by different opinions; I am strong in my faith.

| 220 |

Throw off your old sinful nature and your former way of life, which is corrupted by lust and deception. Instead, let the Spirit renew your thoughts and attitudes. Put on your new nature, created to be like God—truly righteous and holy.

EPHESIANS 4:22–24 NLT

Jesus gives me a new spirit of holiness that helps adjust my thoughts and attitude.

| 221 |

And I will make an everlasting covenant with them:
I will never stop doing good for them. I will put a
desire in their hearts to worship me, and they will
never leave me.

JEREMIAH 32:40 NLT

Even when I feel unfaithful in my
spiritual life, God is still faithful and still
loves me.

| 222 |

A fool gives full vent to his spirit, but a wise man
quietly holds it back.

PROVERBS 29:11 ESV

I don't let my emotions control me;
instead, I resolve things wisely.

| 223 |

For everything there is a season, a time for every activity under heaven. A time to cry and a time to laugh. A time to grieve and a time to dance.

ECCLESIASTES 3:1, 4 NLT

God gives me the patience to wait on new horizons in my life, because I know that His timing is perfect.

| 224 |

For God has not given us a spirit of fear and timidity, but of power, love, and self-discipline.

2 TIMOTHY 1:7 NLT

I don't ever need to feel self-conscious or fearful; God gives me the ultimate confidence!

| 225 |

For God saved us and called us to live a holy life. He did this, not because we deserved it, but because that was his plan from before the beginning of time—to show us his grace through Christ Jesus.

2 TIMOTHY 1:9 NLT

It was always God's desire to show me grace and set me apart for His almighty plan.

| 226 |

You have died with Christ, and he has set you free from the spiritual powers of this world. So why do you keep on following the rules of the world?

COLOSSIANS 2:20 NLT

I don't adapt to worldly lifestyles, because Jesus transcends this world's need for acceptance and calls me to be like Him.

| 227 |

I have loved you, my people, with an everlasting
love. With unfailing love I have drawn you to myself.

JEREMIAH 31:3 NLT

When I feel abandoned and lonely,
I can come to Jesus and be loved.

| 228 |

Gently instruct those who oppose the truth. Perhaps
God will change those people's hearts, and they will
learn the truth. Then they will come to their senses
and escape from the devil's trap. For they have been
held captive by him to do whatever he wants.

2 TIMOTHY 2:25–26 NLT

I am a godly witness for Christ to my
friends and those around me.

| 229 |

Tears of joy will stream down their faces, and I will lead them home with great care. They will walk beside quiet streams and on smooth paths where they will not stumble.

JEREMIAH 31:9 NLT

God brings me peace when I am scared; when I am uncertain, He makes sure I don't get confused.

| 230 |

Avoid worthless, foolish talk that only leads to more godless behavior. This kind of talk spreads like cancer.

2 TIMOTHY 2:16–17 NLT

Jesus helps me refrain from gossiping; instead, I encourage others and control the way I talk.

| 231 |

I say to the Lord, "You are my Lord; apart from you I have no good thing."

PSALMS 16:2 NIV

My relationship with Jesus is my most prized possession; I am nothing without Him.

| 232 |

Love bears all things, believes all things, hopes all things, endures all things.

1 CORINTHIANS 13:7 ESV

I choose to be loving, understanding, and look past others' faults, even when my friends are doing things I don't agree with.

| 233 |

You, Lord, keep my lamp burning; my God turns my darkness into light.

PSALMS 18:28 NIV

When my future seems insecure or lost, I know that Jesus will lead and guide me in light.

| 234 |

Likewise, you who are younger, be subject to the elders. Clothe yourselves, all of you, with humility toward one another, for "God opposes the proud but gives grace to the humble."

1 PETER 5:5 ESV

Jesus asks me to be submissive to my parents or guardians, knowing that God is caring for me through them.

| 235 |

May these words of my mouth and this meditation of my heart be pleasing in your sight, Lord, my Rock and my Redeemer.

PSALMS 19:14 NIV

It's such a privilege to know Jesus; I know my devotion to Him is precious.

| 236 |

Think about Jesus. He held on patiently while sinful men were doing evil things against him. Look at Jesus's example so that you will not get tired and stop trying.

HEBREWS 12:3 ICB

When people do things that accidentally hurt my feelings, Jesus's example encourages me to be strong and gracious.

| 237 |

Because of my integrity you uphold me and set me in your presence forever.

PSALMS 41:12 NIV

I act with integrity at school and work, knowing that Jesus will be pleased with me.

| 238 |

He gave himself for us so he might pay the price to free us from all evil and to make us pure people who belong only to him—people who are always wanting to do good deeds.

TITUS 2:14 NCV

I do good deeds, because Jesus set me free from sin.

| 239 |

By day the Lord directs his love, at night his song is with me—a prayer to the God of my life.

PSALMS 42:8 NIV

God's love and thoughts are with me day and night; no matter where I am, He is with me.

| 240 |

Greater love has no one than this, that someone lay down his life for his friends.

JOHN 15:13 ESV

I learn about true love through the selflessness of my relationships with others.

| 241 |

God is our refuge and strength, an ever-present help in trouble. Therefore we will not fear, though the earth give way and the mountains fall into the heart of the sea, though its waters roar and foam and the mountains quake with their surging.

PSALMS 46:1–3 NIV

Even when life feels hard and my future is unknown, God makes me brave!

| 242 |

The Lord is the everlasting God, the Creator of all the earth. He never grows weak or weary. No one can measure the depths of his understanding. He gives power to the weak and strength to the powerless.

ISAIAH 40:28–29 NLT

Jesus never gets tired, and He passes on His immeasurable strength to me whenever I need it most.

| 243 |

*A foolish person enjoys doing wrong. But a person
with understanding enjoys doing what is wise.*

PROVERBS 10:23 ICB

When I see others doing wrong on
social media, I don't join in; I act wisely.

| 244 |

*Love is patient and kind; love does not envy or boast;
it is not arrogant or rude. It does not insist on its own
way; it is not irritable or resentful; it does not rejoice
at wrongdoing, but rejoices with the truth.*

1 CORINTHIANS 13:4–6 ESV

Jesus teaches me about the kind of
love that results in lasting relationships.

| 245 |

Keep me as the apple of your eye; hide me in the shadow of your wings from the wicked who are out to destroy me, from my mortal enemies who surround me.

PSALMS 17:8–9 NIV

When I am surrounded by people and situations that seem like enemies, Jesus rescues me!

| 246 |

Little children, let us not love in word or talk but in deed and in truth.

1 JOHN 3:18 ESV

God doesn't want me to just say that I love others; He want me to prove it.

| 247 |

The Lord your God is in your midst, a mighty one who will save; he will rejoice over you with gladness; he will quiet you by his love; he will exult over you with loud singing.

ZEPHANIAH 3:17 ESV

Jesus shows His love and joy to me so that I will know how treasured I am.

| 248 |

But the Lord is faithful, and he will strengthen you and protect you from the evil one.

2 THESSALONIANS 3:3 NIV

When I encounter temptations that seem stronger than me, I call on Jesus to strengthen me.

| 249 |

God blesses those who patiently endure testing and temptation. Afterward they will receive the crown of life that God has promised to those who love him.

JAMES 1:12 NLT

God blesses me with wisdom and grace when I bear my difficulties with patience.

| 250 |

Humble yourselves, therefore, under the mighty hand of God so that at the proper time he may exalt you, casting all your anxieties on him, because he cares for you.

1 PETER 5:6–7 ESV

When I submit my life to Jesus and give Him all my cares and worries, He blesses me.

| 251 |

Why, my soul, are you downcast? Why so disturbed within me? Put your hope in God, for I will yet praise him, my Savior and my God.

PSALMS 42:5 NIV

When I have a heart of praise, even if I'm feeling down and sad, God gives me hope!

| 252 |

Whoever desires to love life and see good days, let him keep his tongue from evil and his lips from speaking deceit; let him turn away from evil and do good; let him seek peace and pursue it.

1 PETER 3:10–11 ESV

Jesus wants me to pursue a peaceful life focused on doing good to others and living for Christ.

|253|

I will thank you, Lord, among all the people. I will sing your praises among the nations. For your unfailing love is higher than the heavens. Your faithfulness reaches to the clouds.

PSALMS 108:3–4 NLT

I always go to Jesus with a heart that's thankful for all He's done for me.

|254|

They stumble because they do not obey God's word, and so they meet the fate that was planned for them. But you are not like that, for you are a chosen people . . . God's very own possession. As a result, you can show others the goodness of God, for he called you out of the darkness into his wonderful light.

1 PETER 2:8–9 NLT

I choose to remain a child of God and an example of light, even when my friends fall into sin.

| 255 |

How amazing are the deeds of the Lord! All who delight in him should ponder them. Everything he does reveals his glory and majesty. His righteous-ness never fails.

PSALMS 111:2–3 NLT

I am filled with hope for the future because I remember what Jesus has done in my past.

| 256 |

If a man vows a vow to the Lord, or swears an oath to bind himself by a pledge, he shall not break his word. He shall do according to all that proceeds out of his mouth.

NUMBERS 30:2 ESV

When I make a promise to the Lord or anyone else, I keep my word.

| 257 |

Why should the Gentiles say, "So where is their God?"
But our God is in heaven; He does whatever He
pleases.

PSALMS 115:2–3 NKJV

I know that Jesus is all-powerful, so I don't associate with people who say or believe otherwise.

| 258 |

For his eyes are on the ways of a man, and he sees
all his steps.

JOB 34:21 ESV

My focus is always toward Jesus because He sees every direction I take in life.

| 259 |

The Lord is my shepherd; I shall not want. He makes me lie down in green pastures. He leads me beside still waters. He restores my soul. He leads me in paths of righteousness for his name's sake.

PSALMS 23:1–3 ESV

Jesus wants me to have peace and be happy; all I need to do to have them is follow Him.

| 260 |

Even though I walk through the valley of the shadow of death, I will fear no evil, for you are with me; your rod and your staff, they comfort me.

PSALMS 23:4 ESV

God's protection and discipline comfort me when I lose my way; He always draws me home.

| 261 |

*Let your heart therefore be wholly true to the Lord
our God, walking in his statutes and keeping his
commandments, as at this day.*

1 KINGS 8:61 ESV

I can only be all or nothing for Jesus, so
I am wholly devoted to Him!

| 262 |

*Praise the Lord! How joyful are those who fear the
Lord and delight in obeying his commands. Their
children will be successful everywhere; an entire
generation of godly people will be blessed.*

PSALMS 112:1-2 NLT

When I prioritize God's commands, He
brings me satisfaction and blesses my
whole family!

| 263 |

Let the word of Christ dwell in you richly in all wisdom, teaching and admonishing one another in psalms and hymns and spiritual songs, singing with grace in your hearts to the Lord.

COLOSSIANS 3:16 NKJV

God helps me be a light and good example everywhere, even on social media.

| 264 |

Good and upright is the Lord; therefore he instructs sinners in the way. He leads the humble in what is right, and teaches the humble his way. All the paths of the Lord are steadfast love and faithfulness, for those who keep his covenant and his testimonies.

PSALMS 25:8–10 ESV

Jesus teaches me how to live a good life when I am humble and willing to listen.

| 265 |

Dear friends, you already know about this. So be careful. Do not let those evil people lead you away by the wrong they do. Be careful so that you will not fall from your own strong faith. But grow in the grace and knowledge of our Lord and Savior Jesus Christ.

2 PETER 3:17–18 ICB

I remain faithful even when I see others doing wrong on social media or at school.

| 266 |

I have been crucified with Christ. It is no longer I who live, but Christ who lives in me. And the life I now live in the flesh I live by faith in the Son of God, who loved me and gave himself for me.

GALATIANS 2:20 ESV

Since Jesus died to give me life with Him, I do everything out of love for Him.

| 267 |

Vindicate me, O Lord, for I have walked in my integrity, and I have trusted in the Lord without wavering. Prove me, O Lord, and try me; test my heart and my mind. For your steadfast love is before my eyes, and I walk in your faithfulness.

PSALMS 26:1–3 ESV

I walk solidly with Jesus; I am immovable with my convictions.

| 268 |

I have fought the good fight, I have finished the race, I have kept the faith.

2 TIMOTHY 4:7 ESV

I choose to persevere in my faith and not become worldly, even when it is difficult.

| 269 |

Praise the Lord, all you nations. Praise him, all you people of the earth. For his unfailing love for us is powerful; The Lord's faithfulness endures forever. Praise the Lord!

PSALMS 117 NLT

I know that there is no end to the great things Jesus's love can bring into my life.

| 270 |

A person's wisdom yields patience; it is to one's glory to overlook an offense.

PROVERBS 19:11 NIV

I am wise and treat people patiently, even when they do things that bother me.

| 271 |

But they who wait for the Lord shall renew their strength; they shall mount up with wings like eagles; they shall run and not be weary; they shall walk and not faint.

ISAIAH 40:31 ESV

When I choose to wait for God to work in my life, He is strengthening and teaching me to be brave.

| 272 |

Again I say, don't get involved in foolish, ignorant arguments that only start fights. A servant of the Lord must not quarrel but must be kind to everyone, be able to teach, and be patient with difficult people.

2 TIMOTHY 2:23–24 NLT

Arguing with family and friends isn't worthwhile; instead, I can motivate them through my godly example.

| 273 |

Blessed are those who have regard for the weak; the Lord delivers them in times of trouble.

PSALMS 41:1 NIV

When I keep in mind those who are less fortunate than me, I glorify Jesus.

| 274 |

God has freed us from the power of darkness, and he brought us into the kingdom of his dear Son. The Son paid for our sins, and in him we have forgiveness.

COLOSSIANS 1:13–14 NCV

Whenever I do things I am ashamed of, I remember that I have freedom from shame and forgiveness in Jesus.

| 275 |

But God punishes us to help us, so that we can become holy as he is. We do not enjoy punishment. Being punished is painful at the time. But later, after we have learned from being punished, we have peace, because we start living in the right way.

HEBREWS 12:10–11 ICB

Sometimes the difficulties I endure are lessons from God that teach me how to live righteously.

| 276 |

I am an example to many people. You are my strong protection. I am always praising you. All day long I honor you.

PSALMS 71:7–8 ICB

I affect so many people with my godly example, even though I may not always notice it.

| 277 |

*So be careful and do not refuse to listen when
God speaks. They refused to listen to him when he
warned them on earth. And they did not escape.
Now God is warning us from heaven. So it will be
worse for us if we refuse to listen to him.*

HEBREWS 12:25 ICB

I know that Jesus is trying to save me;
whenever He warns me not to do
something, I listen to Him.

| 278 |

*These are the people I am pleased with: those who
are not proud or stubborn and who fear my word.*

ISAIAH 66:2 NCV

When I am humble and listen to others
who are wise, I make Jesus proud.

| 279 |

That is, in Christ God was reconciling the world to himself, not counting their trespasses against them, and entrusting to us the message of reconciliation.

2 CORINTHIANS 5:19 ESV

Jesus does not count any of my sins against me; instead, He sees me as a new person.

| 280 |

Shout to the Lord, all the earth. Serve the Lord with joy. Come before him with singing. Know that the Lord is God. He made us, and we belong to him. We are his people, the sheep he tends.

PSALMS 100:1–3 ICB

Jesus takes care of me and leads me into good things; in return, I serve Him joyfully.

| 281 |

I therefore, a prisoner for the Lord, urge you to walk in a manner worthy of the calling to which you have been called.

EPHESIANS 4:1 ESV

Jesus has called me to a different life than most, and I will be worthy of this calling.

| 282 |

Those who do not do what is right are not children of God. And anyone who does not love his brother is not a child of God. This is the teaching you have heard from the beginning: We must love each other.

1 JOHN 3:10-11 ICB

Some people are very hard to love, but since Jesus loves them, I do, too.

| 283 |

Indeed, all who desire to live a godly life in Christ Jesus will be persecuted, while evil people and impostors will go on from bad to worse, deceiving and being deceived. But as for you, continue in what you have learned and have firmly believed, knowing from whom you learned it.

2 TIMOTHY 3:12–14 ESV

There are so many evil trends, movies, and people, but I make sure not to allow them into my life.

| 284 |

Brothers, I know that I have not yet reached that goal. But there is one thing I always do: I forget the things that are past. I try as hard as I can to reach the goal that is before me.

PHILIPPIANS 3:13 ICB

I just reach for what is ahead of me, leaving behind my past failures.

| 285 |

Wisdom begins with respect for the Lord. Those who obey his orders have good understanding. He should be praised forever.

PSALMS 111:10 ICB

When I obey God's Word, He gives me the wisdom I need to navigate any situation.

| 286 |

Beloved, I urge you as sojourners and exiles to abstain from the passions of the flesh, which wage war against your soul.

1 PETER 2:11 ESV

I stand strong against the sinful or sexual desires that are constantly trying to bring me down.

| 287 |

Children, obey your parents in everything, for this pleases the Lord.

COLOSSIANS 3:20 ESV

I honor and obey my parents or guardians in everything, because it makes Jesus happy.

| 288 |

In every way be an example of doing good deeds. When you teach, do it with honesty and seriousness. Speak the truth so that you cannot be criticized. Then those who are against you will be ashamed because there is nothing bad to say about us.

TITUS 2:7–8 NCV

I make sure to be a good example for my friends, so that they only have good things to say about me.

| 289 |

Looking to Jesus, the founder and perfecter of our faith, who for the joy that was set before him endured the cross, despising the shame, and is seated at the right hand of the throne of God.

HEBREWS 12:2 ESV

I know Jesus will give me the faith to endure serious hardship because He has endured the same.

| 290 |

Lord God, you are my hope. I have trusted you since I was young. I have depended on you since I was born. You have been my help from the day I was born. I will always praise you.

PSALMS 71:5–6 ICB

I start my journey with the Lord while I am still young, so I do not depart from it later.

| 291 |

Always be full of joy in the Lord. I say it again—
rejoice! Let everyone see that you are considerate in
all you do. Remember, the Lord is coming soon.

PHILIPPIANS 4:4–5 NLT

Time is short, so I am always thankful
and joyful, and I make sure everyone
knows I serve a good God.

| 292 |

God, your justice reaches to the skies. You have done
great things. God, there is no one like you. You have
given me many troubles and bad times. But you
will give me life again. When I am almost dead,
you will keep me alive. You will make me greater
than ever. And you will comfort me again.

PSALMS 71:19–21 ICB

God gives me difficulties to allow my
strength to grow, and He will always
rescue me at the perfect time.

| 293 |

Even a child makes himself known by his acts, by whether his conduct is pure and upright.

PROVERBS 20:11 ESV

My actions always reflect my character, so I will make sure to always act as a woman after God's heart!

| 294 |

Do not say, "I am only a youth"; for to all to whom I send you, you shall go, and whatever I command you, you shall speak. Do not be afraid of them, for I am with you to deliver you, declares the Lord.

JEREMIAH 1:7–8 ESV

It doesn't matter that I'm young; I follow Jesus, no matter what the cost.

| 295 |

Religion that is pure and undefiled before God, the Father, is this: to visit orphans and widows in their affliction, and to keep oneself unstained from the world.

JAMES 1:27 ESV

God is honored when I bless those in need with my time and stay away from worldly things.

| 296 |

I lay down and slept, yet I woke up in safety, for the Lord was watching over me. I am not afraid of ten thousand enemies who surround me on every side.

PSALMS 3:5–6 NLT

When I am tired of all the things coming against me, I rest in Jesus.

| 297 |

So let us be thankful because we have a kingdom that cannot be shaken. We should worship God in a way that pleases him. So let us worship him with respect and fear.

HEBREWS 12:28 ICB

I praise Jesus, knowing that nothing in this world can shake my resolve or my walk with Christ.

| 298 |

You can be sure of this: The Lord set apart the godly for himself. The Lord will answer when I call to him.

PSALMS 4:3 NLT

Jesus has a purpose and plan for my life, so He never stays silent when I need Him.

| 299 |

Get up and shine, because your light has come, and the glory of the Lord shines on you. Darkness now covers the earth; deep darkness covers her people. But the Lord shines on you, and people see his glory around you.

ISAIAH 60:1–2 NCV

God's light and love radiates from my heart; even those who live in sin notice it.

| 300 |

Lord, listen to my words. Understand my sadness. Listen to my cry for help, my King and my God, because I pray to you. Lord, every morning you hear my voice. Every morning, I tell you what I need, and I wait for your answer.

PSALMS 5:1–3 NCV

I tell Jesus everything, because He is my best friend and understands me perfectly.

| 301 |

You have become weak. So make yourselves strong again. Keep on the right path so the weak will not stumble but rather be strengthened.

HEBREWS 12:12–13 ICB

Instead of following a sinful path that I know is wrong, I stay strong and do what is right.

| 302 |

The sun will no longer be your light during the day nor will the brightness from the moon be your light, because the Lord will be your light forever. . . . Your sun will never set again, and your moon will never be dark, because the Lord will be your light forever, and your time of sadness will end.

ISAIAH 60:19–20 NCV

My life might have many seasons of sadness, but God will always be my light and hope.

|303|

So always be ready, because you don't know the day your Lord will come . . . you also must be ready, because the Son of Man will come at a time you don't expect him.

MATTHEW 24:42, 44 NCV

The things of this world are temporary, so I don't waste my time with things that don't glorify Jesus.

|304|

When I felt safe, I said, "I will never fear." Lord, in your kindness you made my mountain safe. But when you turned away, I was frightened.

PSALMS 30:6–7 NCV

I am always safe in His arms when I allow myself to be held by Jesus.

| 305 |

So then, my beloved brethren, let every man be swift to hear, slow to speak, slow to wrath; for the wrath of man does not produce the righteousness of God.

JAMES 1:19–20 NKJV

Instead of being quick to judge, I listen for what Jesus wants me to say and do.

| 306 |

The Lord makes me very happy; all that I am rejoices in my God. He has covered me with clothes of salvation and wrapped me with a coat of goodness, like a bridegroom dressed for his wedding, like a bride dressed in jewels.

ISAIAH 61:10 NCV

God goes above and beyond to make me feel loved and special; that's why my whole being praises Him.

| 307 |

Don't sin by letting anger control you. Think about it overnight and remain silent.

PSALMS 4:4 NLT

When things feel out of control, I don't react in anger; I am peaceful and let Jesus control the outcome of my situations.

| 308 |

Lord, I have heard the news about you; I am amazed at what you have done. Lord, do great things once again in our time; make those things happen again in our own days. Even when you are angry, remember to be kind.

HABAKKUK 3:2 NCV

I pray for my country and my friends to know God's power and love like I do.

| 309 |

Then your light will shine like the dawn, and your wounds will quickly heal. Your God will walk before you, and the glory of the Lord will protect you from behind. Then you will call out, and the Lord will answer. You will cry out, and he will say, "Here I am."

ISAIAH 58:8–9 NCV

When I am sick or going through physical pain, God heals and protects me.

| 310 |

And when a person knows the right thing to do, but does not do it, then he is sinning.

JAMES 4:17 ICB

I walk on God's path of righteousness because in my heart I know what is right.

| 311 |

And the Lord said: "Because this people draw near with their mouth and honor me with their lips, while their hearts are far from me, and their fear of me is a commandment taught by men."

ISAIAH 29:13 ESV

I watch out for fake Christians, so that I remain strong without slipping into sin.

| 312 |

The Lord is good, a stronghold in the day of trouble; he knows those who take refuge in him.

NAHUM 1:7 ESV

When I feel I'm in trouble or struggling, Jesus is my safe place; He gives me hope.

| 313 |

In their hearts humans plan their course, but the Lord establishes their steps.

PROVERBS 16:9 NIV

I plan out my life according to God's direction and ask Him to lead my way.

| 314 |

They kept demanding an answer, so he stood up again and said, "All right, but let the one who has never sinned throw the first stone!"

JOHN 8:7 NLT

I am gracious to people who aren't perfect, because I am a sinner, too.

| 315 |

I tell you the truth, my Father will give you anything you ask for in my name. Until now you have not asked for anything in my name. Ask and you will receive, so that your joy will be the fullest possible joy.

JOHN 16:23–24 NCV

Jesus wants to give me good things in life, and all I need to do to get them is ask!

| 316 |

Pay careful attention to your own work, for then you will get the satisfaction of a job well done, and you won't need to compare yourself to anyone else. For we are each responsible for our own conduct.

GALATIANS 6:4–5 NLT

I don't compare my success to others around me, in life or at school; instead, I just make sure my work is done well.

| 317 |

If you stop making trouble for others, if you stop using cruel words and pointing your finger at others, if you feed those who are hungry and take care of the needs of those who are troubled, then your light will shine in the darkness, and you will be bright like sunshine at noon.

ISAIAH 58:9–10 NCV

I choose to be kind and treat others without judgment, knowing that I shine with God's grace.

| 318 |

You can enter God's Kingdom only through the narrow gate. The highway to hell is broad, and its gate is wide for the many who choose that way. But the gateway to life is very narrow and the road is difficult, and only a few ever find it.

MATTHEW 7:13–14 NLT

It is easy to follow the path of sinners, but it leads to destruction; God's path is difficult but leads to life.

| 319 |

Do not remember the sins and wrong things I did when I was young. But remember to love me always because you are good, Lord.

PSALMS 25:7 NCV

Even when I make immature choices at school, God loves me and forgives me.

| 320 |

If the world hates you, remember that it hated me first. If you belonged to the world, it would love you as it loves its own. But I have chosen you out of the world, so you don't belong to it.

JOHN 15:18–19 NCV

I don't engage in worldly activities, because I am different from this world; I belong to Jesus!

| 321 |

Whoever walks with the wise becomes wise, but the companion of fools will suffer harm.

PROVERBS 13:20 ESV

I choose my friends wisely, so that I can make sure I don't associate with people who will hinder me.

| 322 |

But the Lord said to Samuel, "Don't judge by his appearance or height, for I have rejected him. The Lord doesn't see things the way you see them. People judge by outward appearance, but the Lord looks at the heart."

1 SAMUEL 16:7 NLT

God does not look at my appearance or strength; He sees me for my heart and spirit.

| 323 |

*Remain in me, and I will remain in you. A branch
cannot produce fruit alone but must remain in the
vine. In the same way, you cannot produce fruit
alone but must remain in me.*

JOHN 15:4 NCV

When I stay close to Jesus, He works
through me to accomplish great things.

| 324 |

*Study this Book of Instruction continually. Meditate
on it day and night so you will be sure to obey everything written in it. Only then will you prosper and
succeed in all you do.*

JOSHUA 1:8 NLT

When I study God's Word and
apply it to my life, I am successful in
everything I do.

| 325 |

This God—his way is perfect; the word of the Lord proves true; he is a shield for all those who take refuge in him.

PSALMS 18:30 ESV

The Lord protects and harbors me when I run to Him; He doesn't let me down.

| 326 |

The grass withers and the flowers fade, but the word of our God stands forever.

ISAIAH 40:8 NLT

Some things in life are only temporary, but God's mighty Word will stand firm forever, so I cling to it tightly.

| 327 |

With my whole heart I seek you; let me not wander from your commandments! I have stored up your word in my heart, that I might not sin against you.

PSALMS 119:10–11 ESV

I avoid sinning by reading God's Word and staying true to His commands.

| 328 |

Look up into the heavens. Who created all the stars? He brings them out like an army, one after another, calling each by its name. Because of his great power and incomparable strength, not a single one is missing.

ISAIAH 40:26 NLT

Like the stars in the sky, I was made by my powerful Creator; He won't let me slip out of His hands.

| 329 |

You keep track of all my sorrows. You have collected all my tears in your bottle. You have recorded each one in your book. My enemies will retreat when I call to you for help. This I know: God is on my side!

PSALMS 56:8-9 NLT

Today I release my fears and sorrows, assured that God knows me so intricately that He even saves my tears.

| 330 |

Hatred stirs up trouble. But love forgives all wrongs.

PROVERBS 10:12 ICB

When I get into arguments with my friends, I choose to let go of my anger and be forgiving.

| 331 |

Finally, brothers and sisters, whatever is true, whatever is noble, whatever is right, whatever is pure, whatever is lovely, whatever is admirable—if anything is excellent or praiseworthy—think about such things.

PHILIPPIANS 4:8 NIV

I choose to focus on good and godly things instead of the negativity that spreads quickly on social media.

| 332 |

Jesus said to them, "I am the bread of life; whoever comes to me shall not hunger, and whoever believes in me shall never thirst."

JOHN 6:35 ESV

When I get tired of doing the same things day in and day out, Jesus sustains me with His love and grace.

|333|

I cry out to God Most High, to the God who does everything for me. He sends help from heaven and saves me. He punishes those who chase me. God sends me his love and truth.

PSALMS 57:2–3 NCV

I call out to God whenever I need help because I know He does everything for me.

|334|

Therefore if you have any encouragement from being united with Christ, if any comfort from his love, if any common sharing in the Spirit, if any tenderness and compassion, then make my joy complete by being like-minded, having the same love, being one in spirit and of one mind.

PHILIPPIANS 2:1–2 NIV

Jesus wants me to be open with my faith and share the encouragement He gives me with others.

| 335 |

Whom have I in heaven but you? And earth has nothing I desire besides you. My flesh and my heart may fail, but God is the strength of my heart and my portion forever.

PSALMS 73:25–26 NIV

I trust in the Lord in times when everything seems like it won't work out and my strength isn't enough.

| 336 |

And remember that the heavenly Father to whom you pray has no favorites. He will judge or reward you according to what you do. So you must live in reverent fear of him during your time here as "temporary residents."

1 PETER 1:17 NLT

Jesus will never compare my walk of faith to someone else's, because my relationship with Him is unique.

| 337 |

Praise the Lord! For it is good to sing praises to our God; For it is pleasant, and praise is beautiful.

PSALMS 147:1 NKJV

My inner beauty shines brighter when I praise the Lord with my heart!

| 338 |

The fear of the Lord is the beginning of knowledge; fools despise wisdom and instruction.

PROVERBS 1:7 ESV

I listen to Jesus, my teachers, and my parents or guardians for instruction, because when I do, I submit to God instead of my own pride.

| 339 |

You will call, and I will answer you; you will desire the creature your hands have made. Then you will count my steps, but you will not keep track of my sin. My wrongs will be closed up in a bag, and you will cover up my sin.

JOB 14:15–17 NCV

Jesus does not ever count my sins against me; instead, He forgives me and helps me move on.

| 340 |

When troubles of any kind come your way, consider it an opportunity for great joy. For you know that when your faith is tested, your endurance has a chance to grow. So let it grow, for when your endurance is fully developed, you will be perfect and complete, needing nothing.

JAMES 1:2–4 NLT

My difficult circumstances give me character and perseverance, and they make me stronger for my future.

|341|

May the Lord answer you in times of trouble. May he give you what you want. May all your plans succeed.

PSALMS 20:1, 4 ICB

When I put God first and let Him direct my steps, He makes me successful and blesses me.

|342|

Yes, everyone who continues asking will receive. He who continues searching will find. And he who continues knocking will have the door opened for him.

MATTHEW 7:8 ICB

When I pray, good things happen; God opens the heavens to hear me and pours out His help.

| 343 |

Remain in me and follow my teachings. If you do this, then you can ask for anything you want, and it will be given to you. I loved you as the Father loved me. Now remain in my love.

JOHN 15:7, 9 ICB

When I let my soul rest in Jesus and not earthly things, He gives me my heart's desires.

| 344 |

So I tell you: Live by following the Spirit. Then you will not do what your sinful selves want. Our sinful selves want what is against the Spirit, and the Spirit wants what is against our sinful selves. The two are against each other, so you cannot do just what you please.

GALATIANS 5:16–17 NCV

When I live for Jesus and follow His Spirit, I am not susceptible to my sinful nature.

| 345 |

God is working in you to help you want to do and be able to do what pleases him.

PHILIPPIANS 2:13 NCV

Jesus is working in me and for me, even at times when I don't feel like persevering or being strong.

| 346 |

Good people bring good things out of the good they stored in their hearts. But evil people bring evil things out of the evil they stored in their hearts. People speak the things that are in their hearts.

LUKE 6:45 NCV

I open myself up to Jesus to transform my heart each day, so that I produce good things in my life.

| 347 |

We pray that you will also have great wisdom and understanding in spiritual things so that you will live the kind of life that honors and pleases the Lord in every way. You will produce fruit in every good work and grow in the knowledge of God.

COLOSSIANS 1:9–10 NCV

Every day I strive to understand God's Word, so that I can live a life that pleases Him.

| 348 |

God will strengthen you with his own great power so that you will not give up when troubles come, but you will be patient.

COLOSSIANS 1:11 NCV

When I go through turbulent times, God gives me the patience to deal with my problems.

| 349 |

Turn to me and be gracious to me, for I am lonely and afflicted. The troubles of my heart are enlarged; bring me out of my distresses. Consider my affliction and my trouble, and forgive all my sins.

PSALMS 25:16–18 ESV

Jesus is always near and listens when I am having bad days at school or at home.

| 350 |

You have this faith and love because of your hope, and what you hope for is kept safe for you in heaven. You learned about this hope when you heard the message about the truth, the Good News that was told to you.

COLOSSIANS 1:5–6 NCV

I trust in God's timing, knowing that God has good things saved for me in Heaven.

| 351 |

Then my people, who are called by my name, will be sorry for what they have done. They will pray and obey me and stop their evil ways. If they do, I will hear them from heaven. I will forgive their sin, and I will heal their land.

2 CHRONICLES 7:14 ICB

Since Jesus has given me a new life of grace, I choose to walk away from temptation or sin.

| 352 |

You were cleansed from your sins when you obeyed the truth, so now you must show sincere love to each other as brothers and sisters. Love each other deeply with all your heart.

1 PETER 1:22 NLT

I am able to deeply and sincerely love those around me because of the mercy God has shown me.

| 353 |

*But I will sing about your strength. In the morning
I will sing about your love. You are my defender, my
place of safety in times of trouble. God, my strength,
I will sing praises to you. God, my defender, you are
the God who loves me.*

PSALMS 59:16–17 NCV

When I feel abandoned by my friends,
God reminds me that He is my safe
place and best friend.

| 354 |

*His divine power has granted to us all things that
pertain to life and godliness, through the knowledge of him who called us to his own glory and
excellence.*

2 PETER 1:3 ESV

God's powerful example teaches me
everything I need to live a godly life.

| 355 |

*In all things I have shown you that by working hard
in this way we must help the weak and remember
the words of the Lord Jesus, how he himself said, "It is
more blessed to give than to receive."*

ACTS 20:35 ESV

It blesses my heart to put my energy
into helping those who are hurting,
rather than acquiring new things.

| 356 |

*The Lord is not slow in doing what he promised—the
way some people understand slowness. But God is
being patient with you. He does not want anyone
to be lost. He wants everyone to change his heart
and life.*

2 PETER 3:9 ICB

God is patiently waiting for me to draw
near to Him, so He can bless me with
all He has promised.

| 357 |

It is God who arms me with strength and keeps my way secure. He makes my feet like the feet of a deer; he causes me to stand on the heights.

PSALMS 18:32–33 NIV

Jesus always puts me on a clear path;
I trust Him with my past, present,
and future.

| 358 |

Jesus has the power of God. His power has given us everything we need to live and to serve God. . . . Through his glory and goodness, he gave us the very great and rich gifts he promised us. With those gifts you can share in God's nature. And so the world will not ruin you with its evil desires.

2 PETER 1:3–4 ICB

Jesus gave me many different abilities;
these gifts not only bless others, but
also keep me close to Jesus.

| 359 |

I will look to the Lord for help. I will wait for God to save me. My God will hear me. Enemy, don't laugh at me. I have fallen, but I will get up again. I sit in the shadow of trouble now. But the Lord will be a light for me.

MICAH 7:7–8 ICB

The Lord lifts me up and guides me through any rough patches I might experience in life.

| 360 |

Stay awake and pray for strength against temptation. The spirit wants to do what is right, but the body is weak.

MATTHEW 26:41 NCV

I stay vigilant against the devil and temptation, because I know that my resolve is strong but my flesh is weak.

| 361 |

You will have mercy on us again; you will conquer our sins. You will throw away all our sins into the deepest part of the sea.

MICAH 7:19 NCV

When I feel like I have a specific sin that I can't conquer on my own, I know that Jesus has the strength to conquer it for me.

| 362 |

Obey your leaders and submit to them, for they are keeping watch over your souls, as those who will have to give an account. Let them do this with joy and not with groaning, for that would be of no advantage to you.

HEBREWS 13:17 ESV

I listen and submit to my parents or guardians and spiritual leaders because I know they want what's best for me.

|363|

For the time is coming when people will not endure sound teaching, but having itching ears they will accumulate for themselves teachers to suit their own passions. . . . As for you, always be sober-minded, endure suffering, do the work of an evangelist, fulfill your ministry.

2 TIMOTHY 4:3, 5 ESV

I look to God for my standards of good behavior instead of trying to find people to validate any sin for me.

|364|

And I am certain that God, who began the good work within you, will continue his work until it is finally finished on the day when Christ Jesus returns. . . .
I pray that your love will overflow more and more, and that you will keep on growing in knowledge and understanding.

PHILIPPIANS 1:6, 9 NLT

God is not finished with me yet; I am a beautiful work in progress!

| 365 |

She is clothed with strength and dignity, and she laughs without fear of the future. When she speaks, her words are wise, and she gives instructions with kindness.

PROVERBS 31:25–26 NLT

Jesus makes me brave and wise; I walk with my head high and my heart open to what the future holds!

Resources

Online Resources

ALovelyCalling.com
Facebook.com/alovelycalling
GirlDefined.com
LiesYoungWomenBelieve.com
ReviveOurHearts.com
ReviveOurHearts.com/resource-library/teenager

Books

And the Bride Wore White: Seven Secrets to Sexual Purity by Dannah Gresh

Don't Give the Enemy a Seat at Your Table by Louie Giglio

Grateful Praise!: A Gratitude Journal for Women of Faith by Lisa Zech

Lies Young Women Believe: And the Truth that Sets Them Free by Nancy Leigh DeMoss and Dannah Gresh

Love Defined: Embracing God's Vision for Lasting Love and Satisfying Relationships by Kristen Clark and Bethany Beal

Shine Bright: 60 Days to Becoming a Girl Defined by God by Kristen Clark and Bethany Beal

Scripture Index

OLD TESTAMENT

Scripture Index *continued*

Scripture Index *continued*

Copyright Notices

Acknowledgments

Every book has an author, and behind that author, a village! I first want to thank my awesome husband, who spent many late nights helping me select Bible verses—I love you. Thank you to my family, who helped babysit and inspired my writing. Thank you to my sweet mother-in-law, Suzie, for all your help with the boys. I am so grateful for all of you and your passion to lift the name of Jesus! But mostly, thank you Father God for yet another opportunity to bring glory to your name!

About the Author

 **Lisa Zech** is the founder of *A Lovely Calling*, a blog and social media community dedicated to ministering to girls and women of all ages and backgrounds who are passionate about God's calling for their lives. The ministry focuses on faith, family, godly womanhood, and Christlike relationships, as well as marriage and motherhood. Lisa lives in the mountainous countryside of Montana with her husband, Dylan, and their four beautiful children.